Killer Whale

by CAROLINE ARNOLD
photographs by RICHARD HEWETT

MORROW JUNIOR BOOKS • New York

SHAMU is a registered trademark of the Busch Entertainment Corporation.

PHOTO CREDITS: Permission to use the following photographs is gratefully acknowledged: Sea World, Inc., pages 9 (photo by Jerry Roberts), 10–11 (photo by Bob Couey), 18, 22–23 (photo by Jerry Roberts).

The text type is 14-point Galliard.

1 2 3 4 5 6 7 8 9 10

Library of Congress Cataloging-in-Publication Data.   Arnold, Caroline.   Killer whale / by Caroline Arnold; photographs by Richard Hewett.   p. cm.   Includes index.   ISBN 0-688-12029-6 (trade)—ISBN 0-688-12030-X (library)   1. Killer whale—Juvenile literature.   2. Killer whale—Training—Juvenile literature.   3. Captive mammals—Juvenile literature.   [1. Killer whale.   2. Whales.   3. Killer whale—Training.   4. Captive wild animals.]   I. Hewett, Richard, ill.   II. Title.   QL737.C432A76   1994   599.5'3—dc20   93-33668   CIP   AC

Acknowledgments

We are grateful to the staff at Sea World of California for their cooperation and assistance on this project. We especially appreciate the help of the curator of animal training, Mike Scarpuzzi, and all of his killer whale trainers; Daniel LeBlanc and Margaret Retzlaff in the public relations office; and Dr. Jim McBain, corporate director of veterinary medicine. We also thank the Cabrillo Museum in San Pedro, California, and longtime friend Don Jim for their assistance. And, as always, we thank our editor, Andrea Curley, for her continued support.

PROPELLED by their powerful tails, the young killer whale and her mother glided gracefully through the salty water. They could see their trainer waiting for them on the other side of the pool. Sleek, strong bodies and well-developed senses help make killer whales the top predators of the sea. These same qualities make them popular at marine parks and aquariums.

One-and-a-half-year-old Takara and her mother, Kasatka, are among five killer whales that live at Sea World in San Diego, California. Several other marine parks in North America, including Sea World of Florida, Ohio, and Texas, also have killer whales. Since few people have the chance to see killer whales in the wild, parks like these provide the opportunity to observe these animals up close and to learn more about their amazing abilities.

Scientists who study killer whales in the wild are learning much about where they live and how they behave. But some questions are hard to answer because it is often difficult to see exactly what killer whales are doing when they are underwater or far away. Captive-born killer whales like Takara provide people with a unique opportunity to study these marine creatures in detail and to find out how their young grow, learn, and behave. As we learn more about killer whales, both in the wild and in captivity, we will be better able to understand their role in the oceans of the world.

The killer whales at Sea World live in huge saltwater pools. People can see the whales as they swim at the surface and underwater. With plenty of room to move around, the killer whales behave in many of the same ways they would in the wild.

Several times each day, the killer whales and their trainers put on a show for visitors. When Takara performs, her stage name is Baby Shamu. (Shamu is the name of a famous Sea World killer whale.)

The original Baby Shamu was born in 1985 at Sea World of Florida and was the first killer whale to be born and successfully raised in captivity. Takara is one of several killer whales that have been born at other Sea World parks since then. All of them are called Baby Shamu when they perform. But when Takara works with her trainers, they call her by her real name.

In the show, the killer whales perform both singly and as a group. The "tricks" they do for the audience are based on their natural behavior. Swimming, sliding, leaping, and diving are activities that wild killer whales do every day as they interact with one another and search for food. After the show, people can see the killer whales up close through the thick plastic sides of their pool.

Killer whales are carnivores, or meat eaters. They cruise the ocean in search of prey, which they kill and eat. That is why they are called killer whales. In the wild, their main food is fish, but they also eat other whales, dolphins, seals, sea lions, walrus, squid, and sometimes seabirds and otters. In one part of the performance, the killer whales slide out onto a shallow platform in the center of the stadium. This is the same way a wild killer whale might slide out of the water onto an ice floe or a beach in pursuit of a seal or a sea lion.

A killer whale pod off the coast of Vancouver Island in western Canada.

Killer whales are found in oceans all over the world, ranging from the icy waters near the poles to regions near the equator. They can be seen both in open water and along coastlines, but they are most common within 500 miles (806.5 kilometers) of land.

In the wild, killer whales live in groups called *pods*. The pod may have fewer than five or as many as twenty or more whales in it. The leader is one of the older females, and other members are her offspring or close relatives. A whale usually lives in its mother's pod for its whole life, and it develops strong ties with the other members.

In the wild, a pod may split into smaller groups, if it grows very large or if the leader dies. Each new pod consists of closely related whales and is led

by one of the older females. Although the pods then hunt and travel separately, they may still meet occasionally and stay together for a short time. Groups of related pods are called *clans*.

In the North Pacific, scientists have found that some groups of killer whales stay in the same general location all the time. They call these *resident pods*. Other groups, which they call *transient pods*, travel more widely. Resident pods, ranging from five to fifty killer whales, are usually larger than transient pods and are mainly fish eaters. Transient pods vary in size from one to seven animals and usually eat larger sea life, such as seals and other whales. Killer whales often hunt in groups. In this way, they can attack and kill creatures that are much larger than they are.

Within each pod there is a social order. Scientists who study killer whales think that such behavior as shoving, leaping out of the water, and splashing are some of the ways in which the whales display their strength and assert their dominance.

The spectacular leap out of the water that most whales do is a behavior called *breaching*. Breaching may be one way in which whales communicate with one another. Whales may also breach in order to knock off tiny animals called parasites that cling to their skin and irritate it. And it is possible that whales sometimes leap out of the water just for fun.

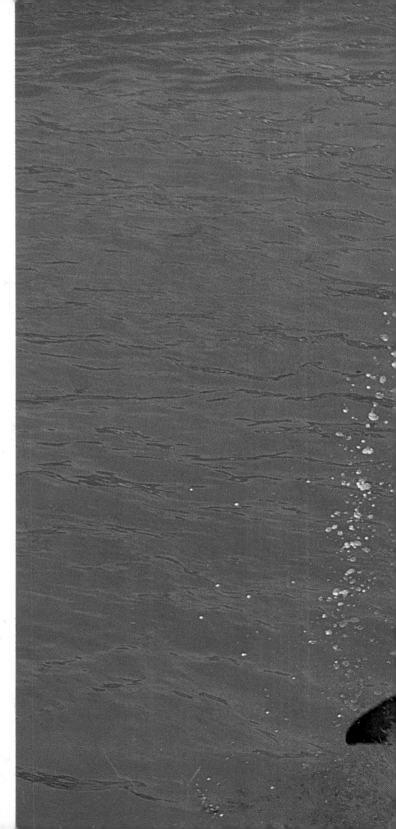

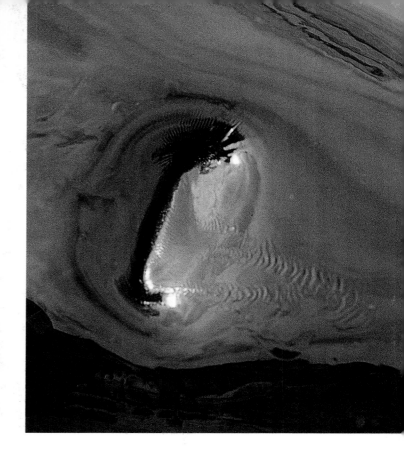

Killer whale blowhole; open (left) and closed (right).

Because whales live in water, people sometimes think they are fish. They are not. Whales are mammals. Both fish and mammals need oxygen to live, but fish can get oxygen directly from the water. Whales cannot do this. They need to breathe air, just like mammals that live on land. A whale breathes through a *blowhole,* an opening located on top of its head. At the blowhole, air goes into the nostrils, which are connected by the windpipe to the whale's lungs.

A whale rises to the surface of the water in order to breathe. First the whale blows a misty plume of air, called a *spout,* out of the blowhole. (A spout is formed by the condensation of moisture in the whale's warm breath when it is expelled into cooler air. It is like the tiny cloud your breath makes when you are outside on a frosty day.) After the whale exhales through the blowhole, it then takes a fresh breath of air. As the whale dives underwater, a special muscle closes

Killer whale spout.

the nostrils inside the blowhole so that water does not get in.

Each species of whale has its own rate of breathing and a characteristic shape and direction of its spout. When killer whales are swimming on the surface, they breathe about twice a minute. When they dive, however, they usually stay underwater for four to five minutes before coming up for air. Occasionally they dive for as long as twelve minutes, and sometimes they have been known to stay underwater for as long as fifteen minutes.

During deep dives special adaptations help a whale to get along without breathing. Its heart slows down. Also, blood flow is reduced to parts of the body that can function without much oxygen. In this way more blood goes to the heart, lungs, and brain so they will continue to be supplied with the oxygen they need.

Many different kinds of whales live in oceans all over the world. The whales range in size from the 130-ton (118.2-metric-ton) blue whale, the largest animal on earth, to the 100-pound (44.4-kilogram) harbor porpoise. All whales belong to the scientific order Cetacea. (Scientists who study whales are called cetologists.) The Cetacean group is divided into two suborders of living whales: the toothed whales, or Odontoceti, and the baleen whales, or Mysticeti. (Members of a third suborder, ancient whales called the Archaeoceti, are all extinct.)

Mysticeti comes from Greek words meaning "mustached whale." Instead of teeth, the whales in the Mysticeti suborder have plates, called *baleen,* that hang down from the upper jaw. The edges of the baleen are fringed and form long flexible brushes. Baleen is made of material similar to that of fingernails. The whales use their baleen to strain small fish, shrimplike animals, and other tiny pieces of food from the water. When the whale eats, it takes in a mouthful of water and food and then uses its tongue to push out the water. Then it swallows the food that was trapped in its baleen.

The baleen whales include the blue, fin, sei, Bryde's, minke, humpback, gray, bowhead, right, and pygmy right whales.

Odontoceti comes from Greek words meaning "toothed whale." Killer whales are one of more than seventy-five species that belong to this suborder. Some other species of toothed whales are the white whale and the pilot whale. All toothed whales are hunters of the sea. A toothed whale has large peg-shaped teeth along its upper and lower jaws. These are used to rip or tear pieces of flesh. Its strong jaws and teeth are good for grabbing and holding food. Toothed whales cannot chew their food. Instead, they swallow it whole or in large pieces.

Baleen and toothed whales differ in other ways as well. Most of the toothed whales are smaller than the baleen whales. They also are more social and usually live together in pods. The toothed whales have only one blowhole, whereas the baleen whales have two—one for each nostril. Another difference between the two types of whales is that male toothed whales are larger than the females, while among baleen whales, the females are larger than the males.

Baleen in the mouth of a California gray whale skeleton (above). Killer whale teeth (below).

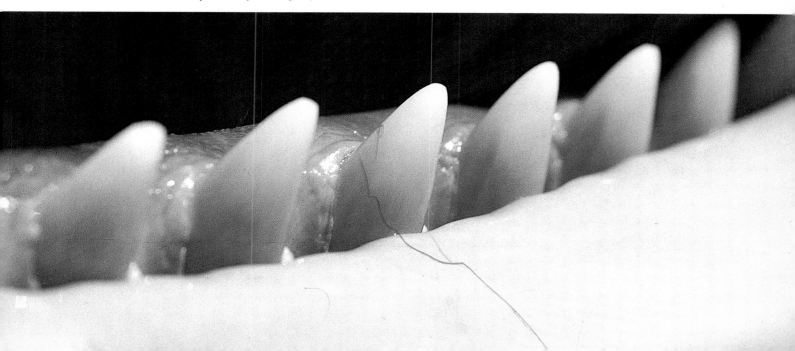

Bottlenose dolphins.

Each suborder of whales is divided into groups called families. (*Family* is the scientific term used for a group of species with similar characteristics.) The killer whale is the largest species in the dolphin family and has the scientific name *Orcinus orca*. Because of this, people sometimes call them orca whales. Some other species in the dolphin family include the Pacific white-sided dolphin, the bottlenose dolphin, and the common dolphin.

An adult male killer whale usually measures from 22 to 27 feet (6.7 to 8.2 meters) long and weighs from 8,000 to 12,000 pounds (3,636.4 to 5,454.5 kilograms). Adult females are 17 to 24 feet (5.2 to 7.3 meters) long and weigh from 3,000 to 8,000 pounds (1,363.6 to 3,636.4 kilograms).

Some killer whales grow even larger. The biggest male ever found was 32 feet (9.8 meters) long and weighed 21,000 pounds (9,545.5 kilograms)! The big-

Killer whales.

gest known female was 28 feet (8.5 meters) and 15,000 pounds (6,818.2 kilograms).

The coloring of male and female killer whales is the same. Both have black backs and tails with a gray patch located behind the tall dorsal fin in the center of the back. (This patch is called the *saddle*.) The dorsal fin and the pectoral flippers on either side of the body are also black. On its underside, the killer whale is white. It also has a white marking above each eye called the *eyespot*.

Although it is easy to see the killer whales in the clear water at a marine park, their coloring helps to hide them as they hunt for food in the ocean. When seen from above, the killer whales' black backs blend into the dark water below. When viewed from below, their white undersides are hard to see against the sky; from the side, their black-and-white coloring resembles dappled sunshine in the water.

Killer whales do not reach their full adult size until they are in their late teens, but they can mate at an earlier age. Females are able to mate when they are about 15 to 16 feet (4.6 to 4.9 meters) long. Males can mate when they reach 18 to 20 feet (5.5 to 6.1 meters) in length. Scientists who study killer whales in the wild have found that females give birth for the first time when they are about fifteen years old.

Although killer whales can mate at any time of year, mating is more common in the summer months. Mating of killer whales has rarely been seen in the wild. However, because females in pods with no adult male members regularly give birth, scientists think that females probably mate with males outside their own pod. A female does not form a lasting relationship with her mate, and she may mate with several different males. When they have finished mating, the male and female no longer stay together. Only the mother killer whale looks after her offspring. A female killer whale is pregnant for seventeen months before giving birth. A baby killer whale is called a *calf*. Kasatka was about fifteen years old when Takara was born, and Takara was her first calf.

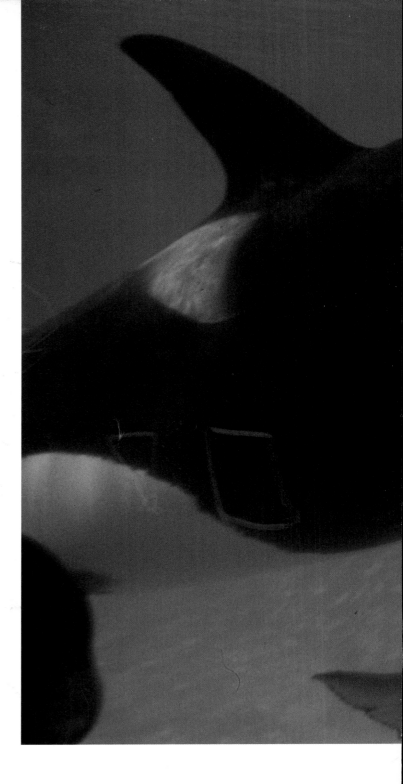

A killer whale mother gives birth to her single calf underwater. The calf may emerge either headfirst or tail first, and as soon as it is born the mother whale pushes it gently toward the surface of the water so it can take its first breath. The mother killer whale watches over her new calf carefully and makes sure that it stays close beside her.

A newborn calf is about 8 feet (2.4 meters) long and weighs about 300 to 400 pounds (136.4 to 181.8 kilograms). Its dorsal fin and tail are soft and flexible, but these stiffen during the calf's first few days. The markings of a killer whale calf are the same as an adult's, although the calf's light areas are sometimes yellow or cream colored. They gradually become white by the time the calf is a year old.

Although Takara could swim as soon as she was born, she was not as strong as the bigger whales. By swimming alongside her mother, she could ride in the wave of water, or *slipstream*, Kasatka made when she swam. In this way, the calf uses less energy, and the mother and baby can keep up with the rest of the pod as the whales move about.

The first food for a killer whale calf is milk, just as it is for other mammals. The mother killer whale's two teats are inside two slits on her underside. A killer whale calf nurses underwater and drinks for about five to ten seconds at a time. It feeds several times an hour, both day and night. As the calf sucks, milk squirts into its mouth.

The milk of a mother killer whale is about 35 percent fat. This is a high percentage of fat compared to the milk of most other mammals. Cow's milk, for instance, is about 3.4 percent fat. When the killer whale calf drinks its mother's milk, the digestive process converts some of the milk fat into body fat. It is stored as a thick layer, called *blubber*, underneath the skin. Fat is a good insulator that helps to keep a killer whale's body heat inside. In this way, the whale stays warm even when it swims in cold water. For wild killer whales, blubber also provides energy during periods when there is no food to eat. Takara's body soon became bigger and rounder as she developed a thick layer of blubber.

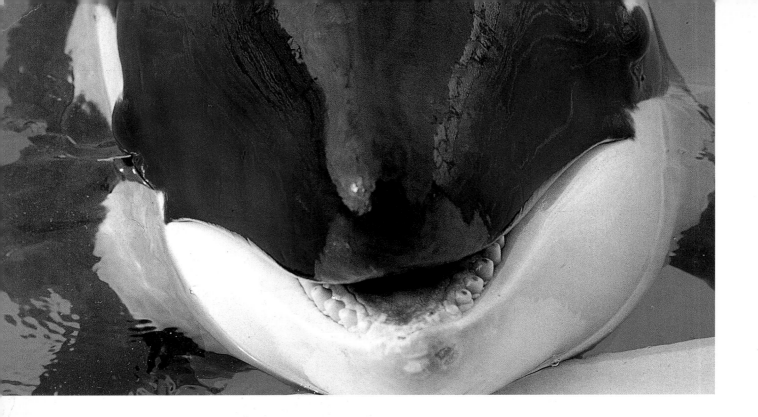

Takara's teeth started to grow in when she was three to four months old. Although she continued to nurse until she was about a year old, she was ready to begin eating solid food.

The number of teeth in killer whales varies among individuals. Usually a whale has between ten and fourteen teeth on each side of the jaw, for a total of forty to fifty-six teeth. The teeth grow throughout a whale's life. By examining the growth layers, scientists can estimate the age of a killer whale.

Killer whales have huge appetites to go with their active life-style. At Sea World, a one-year-old calf eats about 50 to 60 pounds (22.7 to 27.3 kilograms) of fish every day. A large adult killer whale can eat up to 300 pounds (136.4 kilograms) of food each day! The adult whales that live at Sea World eat between 200 and 250 pounds (90.7–113.4 kilograms) each day. Sea World feeds its whales a diet of such fish as smelt, mackerel, herring, and squid plus supplements of vitamins and minerals. The whales are fed numerous meals throughout the day.

Every part of a killer whale's body is adapted to life in the sea and helps to make it a successful predator. Despite its large size, a killer whale is an agile and graceful swimmer. Its sleek torpedo shape is ideal for moving quickly through the water. Strong muscles control the body, and the surrounding water helps to support its enormous weight. With apparent ease a killer whale can twist, turn, twirl, and even swim upside down. Killer whales are among the fastest animals in the sea and can swim at speeds of up to 30 miles (48.4 kilometers) per hour. Usually, though, they swim more slowly, between 2 and 6 miles (3.2–9.7 kilometers) per hour.

Two broad flat lobes at the end of a killer whale's tail are called *flukes*. In a large adult male, they may measure up to 9 feet (2.7 meters) across. These flukes are connected to bones at the base of the spine and are made of tough boneless tissue. By pushing the tail up and down, the flukes push the whale forward through the water. They work in the same way in which flippers help a scuba diver to swim. By holding its flukes down, the whale can also use them as a brake. At the surface of the water, the whale sometimes uses its flukes to splash water, a behavior called *lobtailing*.

Steering and balance are provided by the whale's dorsal fin and pectoral flippers. The *dorsal fin* is the large fin at the center of the whale's back. Dorsal fins vary slightly in shape and are one way in which people can identify individual whales. An adult male has a high straight dorsal fin that may be 6 feet (1.8 meters) tall. The dorsal fin of an adult female is shorter, usually about 3 to 4 feet (.91 to 1.2 meters) tall, and it is often curved back slightly.

Like the flukes, the stiff dorsal fin has no bones. Its strength comes from strong fibers within it. The dorsal fin acts like the keel of a boat and helps to keep the whale from sliding sideways in the water.

A killer whale uses its *pectoral flippers* mainly to steer and stop. These large paddlelike structures are the equivalent of forelimbs in land animals. The bones inside each flipper are somewhat similar to those in a human hand, except that they are much larger and stronger. Thick cartilage pads between the bones act as cushions. The bones are connected by strong tissues and are covered by a thick outer layer of tough skin. The pectoral flippers of a large male killer whale may be 6½ feet (2 meters) long and 4 feet (1.2 meters) wide.

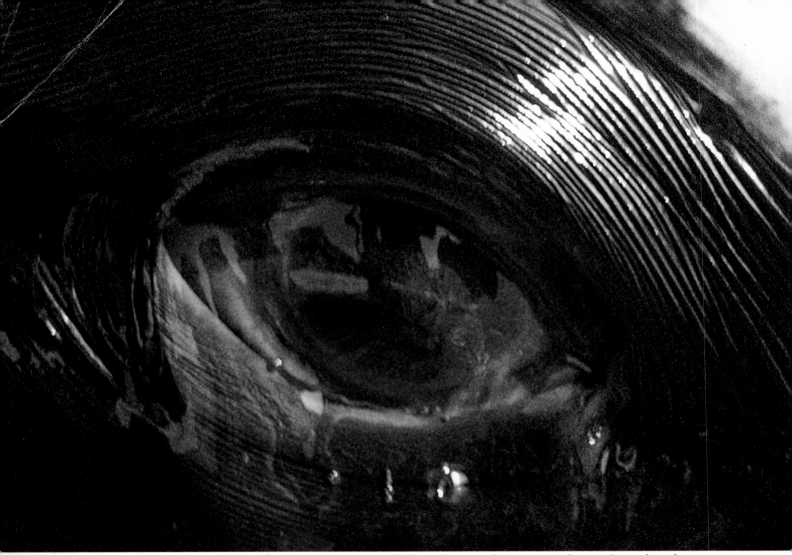

Special glands in the eyelids produce a transparent jellylike substance that protects the eyes from the salty seawater when the whale is underwater.

You may sometimes see a killer whale poke its head straight up out of the water, as if it were standing on its tail. This behavior is called *spyhopping*. When it spyhops, a whale can get a good look around. A killer whale has good eyesight, and in clear coastal waters it can see for distances up to 100 feet (30.5 meters). But when the water is dark or murky, it may be difficult for the whale to see very far, then it must depend on its sense of hearing.

32

Killer whales use a technique called *echolocation,* or sonar, to find their way around in the ocean. To echolocate, the killer whale first makes high-pitched sounds. It then listens to the echoes these sounds make when they bounce off nearby objects, and it uses the sounds to tell the distance, shape, and size of those objects. To the human ear, these noises sound like a series of rapid clicks. The killer whale makes them by forcing air through cavities in its head that are underneath the blowhole.

Inside the bulge on the top of a killer whale's head is a mound of fat called the *melon.* The melon allows the whale to focus high-pitched sounds into a narrow beam and, by doing this, to control the direction of these sound beams with great accuracy. In this way, the whale can precisely locate objects in the water. A young whale like Takara is not able to echolocate as well as the older whales. She will gradually learn by trial and error. Killer whales, bottlenose dolphins, and some of the other toothed whales use echolocation both to navigate and to locate   Baleen whales are not known to have this ability.

Killer whales have a highly developed sense of hearing. The inner ear, which is sensitive to sound, is deep within the whale's head. Although the killer whale has a small external ear opening just above each eye, the channel from the external ear to the inner ear is closed. Instead, sound vibrations in the water pass through the bones and fat in the lower jaw to the killer whale's inner ear.

Sound is an extremely important means of communication for all whales. Sound vibrations travel better in water than they do in air. Scientists who study killer whales can sometimes detect their sounds up to 5 miles (8.1 kilometers) away. Killer whale calls include a combination of clicks, whistles, screeches, and squeals. An individual killer whale may use from seven to seventeen different calls. Members of a pod all use the same set of calls. They use these signals to keep in contact with one another as they travel and forage for food. Calls are also used to identify each whale and to communicate with other pods.

Even before a young killer whale is born, it can hear its mother's calls and so becomes familiar with them. Like humans, birds, and a few other animals, killer whales are able to learn new sounds by imitating what they hear. A young killer whale like Takara learns the "language" of her pod by listening to her mother and trying to copy her sounds.

Scientists who study killer whales in the wild are able to identify pods by their calls. In the same way that people who live in different parts of the world speak with different accents or dialects, the killer whale pods in different parts of the ocean each have their own dialects. Dialects help killer whales to identify members of their own family, and this may help to prevent them from mating with close relatives.

The whales watch their trainers to get directions for what to do.

From the time she was born, Takara accompanied her mother during her training sessions at Sea World. Each day the trainers work with the killer whales to teach them new skills and practice old ones. This gives the whales both exercise and mental stimulation. Trainers work with the whales in and out of the water and use both sounds and hand and body signals to tell the animals what to do. The killer whales learn quickly, and they seem to enjoy performing.

Because the trainers work closely with the whales, they get to know them well. Each whale has its own distinctive markings and its own personality. The trainers and killer whales develop good relationships and learn to trust one another. Even so, the trainers are always careful because they know killer whales are large and powerful and, like all wild animals, can be dangerous.

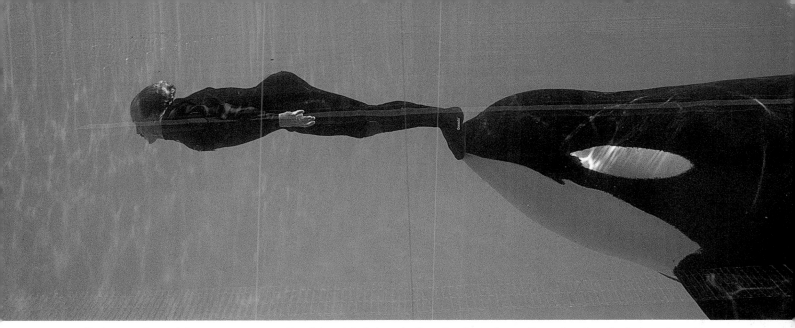

Power and precision are necessary for this trick (above). Just for fun, the trainers let the whales see themselves in a mirror (below).

An important part of the training process is letting the whale know when it has performed well. All of the training at Sea World is based on rewarding the animals for correct behavior. Often the whales are rewarded with fish, but they also enjoy eating ice cubes, having a squirt from a hose, or getting rub-downs. The skin of a killer whale is sensitive to touch. In the wild, killer whales are sometimes seen rubbing themselves on pebble beaches; they appear to like the feel of the smooth stones against their skin.

Early in its training, a killer whale learns that the sound of its trainer's whistle is also a reward. When a whale is performing in the middle of the pool and the trainer is standing at the edge, it is hard for the trainer to give an immediate reward such as a fish. Instead, the trainer blows the whistle to let the whale know exactly which part of its performance was good. In this way, the trainers can shape a complex series of behaviors.

Training helps the staff at Sea World to direct the whales' behavior so that they can care for the animals. Because the trainers spend so much time with the killer whales, they are often the first to notice when a whale is behaving in an unusual way. Trainers work closely with the veterinary staff at the park. Twice a day one of the veterinarians walks around the killer whale enclosure and watches the whales to make sure they seem healthy. The vets also talk to the trainers and read their notes about the killer whales' activities and behav-

ior. When a whale needs to be examined by the vet, the trainer teaches the whale to hold still.

It is difficult for a veterinarian to feel the organs inside a killer whale because they are so well cushioned by the whale's thick blubber. Instead, most of the routine health care is done by analyzing blood and urine samples in the laboratory. The killer whales are trained to give urine samples and to present their flukes for blood sampling. Large blood vessels in the flukes make them a good place from which to draw blood.

When the killer whales are not performing or working with their trainers, they are allowed to rest and swim freely around their enclosure. Killer whales rest by taking short naps. They may rest for just a few minutes or for as long as four hours at a time. To sleep, killer whales float at the surface of the water and close their eyes. They do this both day and night.

As Takara grew older and became more independent, she sometimes played with four-year-old Splash, the other youngster in their group. Young animals play to strengthen their muscles and to develop their coordination. In the wild, young killer whales have been observed chasing, pushing, and splashing one another in what appears to be play behavior. As Takara and Splash swam and jumped together in their pool, they called back and forth to each other.

A young killer whale grows rapidly at first, and by the time it is a year old, it has more than doubled its size. At the age of a year and a half, Takara weighed 1,200 pounds (545.5 kilograms). She will reach her adult size in her middle teenage years.

Researchers believe that the average life span for killer whales is between about twenty-five and thirty-five years. Some killer whales, however, have been known to live eighty years or longer. Corky, a twenty-seven-year-old female, is the oldest killer whale at Sea World of California. With good care, Takara and the other whales at Sea World parks can expect to live long, healthy lives.

Young killer whales in the wild are sometimes attacked by sharks, but adults have no natural enemies except for humans. Fishing nets that trap animals underwater have needlessly killed many whales and dolphins. A further danger is the pollution of the world's oceans.

For thousands of years, whales have been an important resource for people who hunted them for their meat, fat, and bones. Whalers usually prefer to catch the larger baleen whales, but they sometimes catch killer whales, too. Today, the highly mechanized whaling industry threatens many of the larger whales with extinction. Although laws protect many species of whales, enforcing those laws requires the cooperation of nations all over the world.

Marine parks and aquariums let us observe whales at close range and study their behavior. The more we can learn about whales and how they live, the better we will understand how to help protect them and their environment. Killer whales like Takara help us to know this species better and to appreciate the amazing strength and behaviors of these magnificent hunters of the sea.

46

Index

Photographs are in **boldface.**